Plus

First Ladies
Michelle Obama

by Lucia Raatma

Consulting editor: Gail Saunders-Smith, PhD

Consultant: Carl Sferrazza Anthony, Historian
National First Ladies' Library
Canton, Ohio

CAPSTONE PRESS
a capstone imprint

Pebble Plus is published by Capstone Press,
1710 Roe Crest Drive, North Mankato, Minnesota 56003.
www.capstonepub.com

Library of Congress Cataloging-in-Publication Data
Raatma, Lucia.
Michelle Obama / by Lucia Raatma.
p. cm.—(Pebble plus. First ladies)
Summary: "Simple text and photographs describe the life of Michelle Obama"—Provided by publisher.
Includes bibliographical references and index.
ISBN 978-1-4296-5008-3 (library binding)
ISBN 978-1-4296-5599-6 (paperback)
1. Obama, Michelle, 1964– —Juvenile literature. 2. Presidents' spouses—United States—Biography—Juvenile
literature. 3. Legislators' spouses—United States—Biography—Juvenile literature. 4. African American women
lawyers—Illinois—Chicago—Biography—Juvenile literature. I. Title. II. Series.
E909.O24R33 2011
973.932092—dc22
[B]   2009050393

Editorial Credits
Jennifer Besel, editor; Ashlee Suker, designer; Svetlana Zhurkin, media researcher; Eric Manske, production specialist

Photo Credits
Alamy/Jason O. Watson, 16–17; Vespasian, 9
AP Images/Obama for America, 11; Ted S. Warren, 5
Corbis/Brooks Kraft, cover (right)
Getty Images/AFP/Mandel Ngan, 21; AFP/Tim Sloan, 19; Barry Brecheisen, 6–7; Mark Wilson, 1, 12–13
Landov/Chicago Tribune/MCT, 15
Shutterstock/Alaettin Yildirim, 5, 7, 9, 13, 15, 19 (caption plate); antoninaart, cover (left), 1, 10–11, 14–15, 22–23, 24
    (pattern); Gemenacom, 11, 15 (frame)

Note to Parents and Teachers

The First Ladies series supports national history standards related to people and culture. This
book describes and illustrates the life of Michelle Obama. The images support early readers
in understanding the text. The repetition of words and phrases helps early readers learn new
words. This book also introduces early readers to subject-specific vocabulary words, which are
defined in the Glossary section. Early readers may need assistance to read some words and to
use the Table of Contents, Glossary, Read More, Internet Sites, and Index sections of the book.

Printed in Canada.
082013   007675R

Table of Contents

Early Life

Michelle Obama is the first

African-American first lady.

She was born in Chicago,

Illinois, on January 17, 1964.

She grew up with her parents,

Fraser and Marian Robinson,

and her brother, Craig.

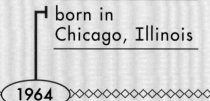

born in
Chicago, Illinois

1964

Michelle and her mother in 2008

The Robinsons lived

in a small apartment.

But they made room

for a piano. Michelle loved

to play. Her mother

had to stop her

from practicing too long.

born in
Chicago, Illinois

1964

Michelle lived with her family in the upstairs apartment in this home.

Michelle was a serious student.

In 1985 she graduated

from Princeton University.

Michelle graduated

from Harvard Law School

in 1988. She became

a lawyer in Chicago.

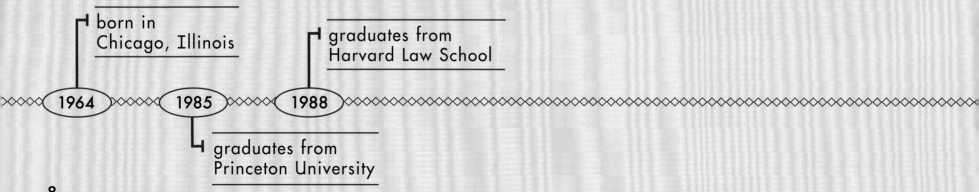

born in
Chicago, Illinois

graduates from
Harvard Law School

1964   1985   1988

graduates from
Princeton University

Harvard Law School

Michelle met Barack Obama
in Chicago. Barack made her
happy, but her job didn't.
Michelle wanted a job that
helped people. She left her
law firm in 1991. Michelle married
Barack on October 3, 1992.

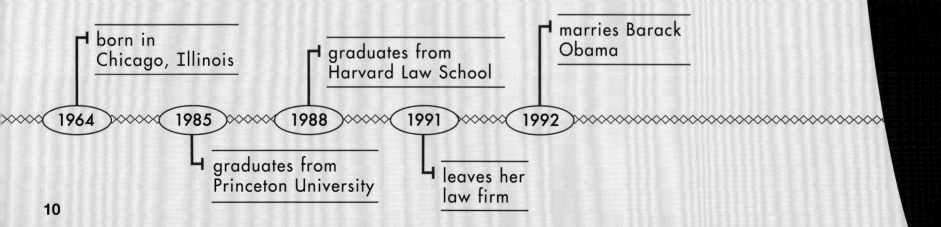

born in
Chicago, Illinois

graduates from
Harvard Law School

marries Barack
Obama

1964   1985   1988   1991   1992

graduates from
Princeton University

leaves her
law firm

Working Mom

Michelle found new jobs. She trained people to be community leaders. She also got doctors to volunteer to help the poor. Michelle felt good that her new jobs helped others.

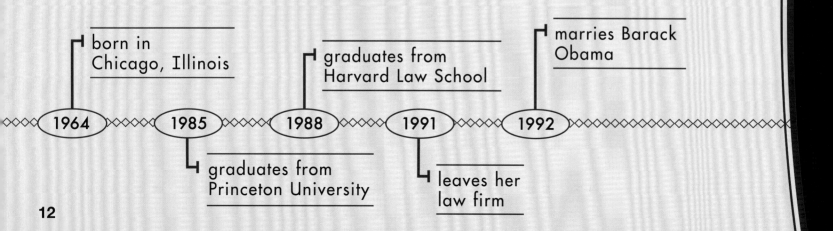

born in
Chicago, Illinois

graduates from
Harvard Law School

marries Barack
Obama

1964   1985   1988   1991   1992

graduates from
Princeton University

leaves her
law firm

As first lady, Michelle continues to encourage doctors to volunteer.

Michelle and Barack have
two daughters, Malia and
Sasha. Michelle planned
her work hours so she
could spend time with them.
Michelle and her daughters
love to read together.

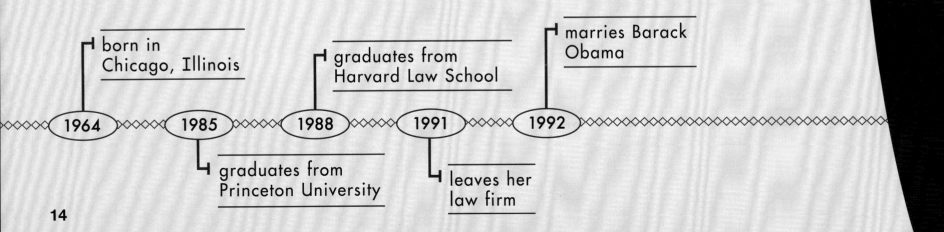

born in
Chicago, Illinois

graduates from
Harvard Law School

marries Barack
Obama

1964   1985   1988   1991   1992

graduates from
Princeton University

leaves her
law firm

Michelle with Sasha
(left) and Malia
(right) in 2004

First Lady

Barack was elected to the U.S. Senate in 2004. In 2007 he decided to run for president. Michelle helped with his campaign. She gave speeches all over the country.

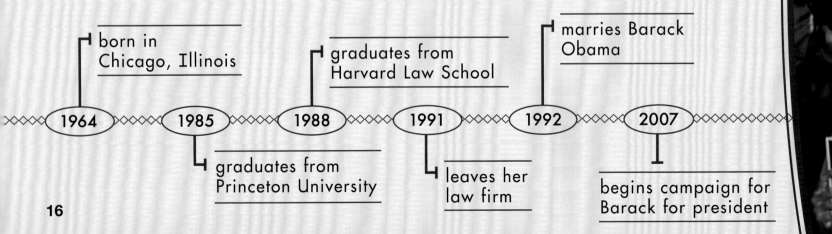

1964	1985	1988	1991	1992	2007
born in Chicago, Illinois		graduates from Harvard Law School		marries Barack Obama	
	graduates from Princeton University		leaves her law firm		begins campaign for Barack for president

In January 2009

Barack became president.

Michelle became first lady.

She grew vegetables

at the White House.

She wanted to remind people

to eat healthy foods.

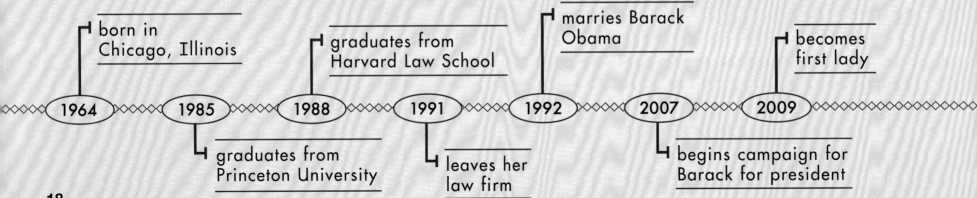

born in
Chicago, Illinois

graduates from
Harvard Law School

marries Barack
Obama

becomes
first lady

1964　1985　1988　1991　1992　2007　2009

graduates from
Princeton University

leaves her
law firm

begins campaign for
Barack for president

Michelle invited students to work in the White House garden.

Carrot
Hercules

As first lady, Michelle travels
the world. She talks to people
about volunteering
in their communities.
She hopes to make the world
better for everyone.

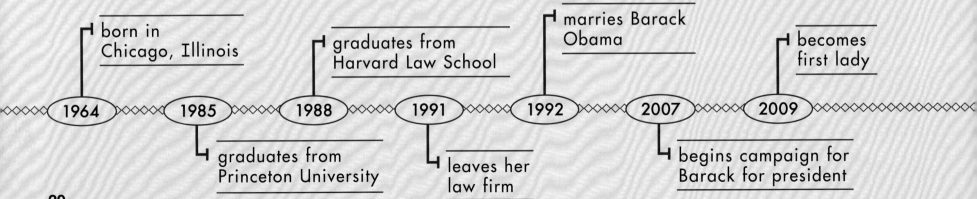

born in
Chicago, Illinois

graduates from
Harvard Law School

marries Barack
Obama

becomes
first lady

1964   1985   1988   1991   1992   2007   2009

graduates from
Princeton University

leaves her
law firm

begins campaign for
Barack for president

Glossary

campaign—an organized effort to win political office

community—a group of people who live in the same area or have something in common

elect—to choose a person for a job or task by voting

first lady—the wife of the president of the United States

law firm—a business where lawyers work

Senate—one part of the Congress, which is a group of people who make laws

volunteer—to offer to do something without pay

Read more

Kennedy, Marge. *Who Works at the White House?* Scholastic News Nonfiction Readers. New York: Children's Press, 2009.

Marks, Jennifer L. *President Barack Obama*. Mankato, Minn.: Capstone Press, 2009.

Nault, Jennifer. *Michelle Obama*. Remarkable People. New York: Weigl Publishers, Inc., 2010.

Internet Sites

FactHound offers a safe, fun way to find Internet sites related to this book. All of the sites on FactHound have been researched by our staff.

Here's all you do:

Visit *www.facthound.com*

FactHound will fetch the best sites for you!

Index

Word Count: 260
Grade: 1
Early-Intervention Level: 20